# THE PEACE OF CHRIST
## Surpassing All Understanding

Loyd L. Fueston, Jr.

*Wipf & Stock*
PUBLISHERS
*Eugene, Oregon*

THE PEACE OF CHRIST
Surpassing All Understanding

I consider that the sufferings of this present time are not worth comparing with the glory that is to be revealed to us. For the creation waits with eager longing for the revealing of the sons of God; for the creation was subjected to futility, not of its own will but by the will of him who subjected it in hope; because the creation itself will be set free from its bondage to decay and obtain the glorious liberty of the children of God. We know that the whole creation has been groaning in travail together until now; and not only the creation but we ourselves who have the first fruits of the Spirit groan inwardly as we wait for adoption as sons, the redemption of our bodies.

---

St. Paul, Romans 8:18-23

# Contents

# Preface

In my first published book, *To See a World in a Grain of Sand*, I claimed that mortal man is born a human animal in a world which is a place of struggle between order and disorder. [I'll refer to this earlier book as simply *World* to save typing.] This book, *The Peace of Christ*, rests upon *World.* While the specifics of my worldview might change over the remaining years of my life, *World* presented the overall framework of my thoughts about Creation and about God as Creator at a certain important time in my life.

In this book, I'll be exploring but one strand of the Good News of Jesus Christ: perfect peace can be realized only in the world of the resurrected. We mortal men can only dimly perceive that perfect peace on this side of the grave. Some of us might even experience that perfect peace for a short while. We can persist in such perfect peace only on the other side of the grave. We know little about that New World to be inhabited by those deemed worthy of participating in the Resurrection. That life will be known to us only when we enter it, but we begin to understand something of the true nature of that perfect order when we name it as the Peace of Christ. We understand better when we pray to God, when we read the Bible, and when we worship Him. All of this should be done even before we enjoy such activities. All of this should be done even before we come to truly love God. All of this should be done out of a sense of justice to our Maker.

We should accept God's gift of peace, first of all because we owe it to Him, but we should realize that when we live in the Peace of Jesus Christ, we'll be sharing the Life of God. This is a pearl of rather great price. We should be selling all we have to obtain this one pearl.

# Introduction

This book is primarily a spiritual work about that perfect order which is the Peace of Christ. It's the only perfect order possible for a mere creature, a mortal man. It's the only true peace and we can enter the realm of this perfect peace only because the Son of God became a man, became one of us, allowing us, His brothers, to join Him in His divine life.

But there's a catch to this gift. To enter this realm of perfect peace, we must become like Christ. We must accept an infusion of grace, divine love focused in particular ways.

In the end, God Himself does the heavy lifting, but He wants us to participate in a task impossible for us: our transformation into beings capable of sharing unending life with His Son. All else being equal, a human animal couldn't possibly love God enough to center his attention upon the Almighty. God Himself must provide the love which we render to Him. A human animal couldn't possibly be at peace for time without end. It's the divine life which itself is peace and we can be at peace only when we share God's life. Without that particular gift, I don't see how creatures such as we are could possibly be happy being at peace for time without end.

Though God gives freely, He expects something out of us. He expects us to pray with Him in various ways, asking Him for what we need or thanking Him for what He has given us. He expects us also to sit quietly with Him, learning how to pray with Him, to listen with Him, to think with Him.

God also expects us to read the Bible, the word He has spoken through His prophets and His evangelists.

The Almighty has also commanded us to worship Him and especially to eat the Body of the Son of God and to drink His Blood in the Eucharistic Rite. Jesus Christ told us that only those who do so have life in them. That is, only those who eat His Body and drink His blood have a share of the divine life, of the dynamic peace which is the interaction of Father and

Son and Holy Spirit. We know that life, that peace, as the Peace of Christ.

## Technical Note

I'm very particular in the way I use the word 'person', a word which must be defined properly to preserve Christian belief in Jesus Christ as true man and true God, one Person – the Son of God, but two natures – human and divine.

We've abused this word, sometimes speaking as if a 'human person' is no more and no less than a 'human being'. Thus we assume that each human being at birth is also a human person. This creates a great problem that's easily seen when we try to answer the question:

> Was Jesus of Nazareth born a human person?

If we say, "Yes," then we either deny He was a divine Person, the Son of God, or else we make the silly claim He was two persons. If we say, "No," we make Him different in His human nature from the rest of us – He wasn't a true man. That is, if we're born as human persons and He wasn't, then His human nature was radically incomplete.

To avoid this problem, I proposed in World that we accept that we're born with only the potential to become persons and I defined a person as having the characteristics of: unity and coherence and completeness. We only acquire those characteristics when we become like Christ, when we let Christ infuse our beings. Accepting this claim forces us to speak of ourselves as human beings or human animals but only as human persons to the extent that we've become Christ-like.

This will be the only time in this book, I'll veer close to a technical philosophical discussion.

## Bibliographical Note

Biblical quotations in this book are drawn from the *Revised Standard Version, Catholic Edition*, 1966 as published by Thomas Nelson Publishers for Ignatius Press.

# 1 Battles Between Order and Disorder

## 1.1 The Universal Battleground

The world is a story told by God in His freely chosen role as Creator of this particular world, as the author of this particular story. Much of this story is unclear to human eyes. Much of this story involves disorder. Pain and suffering is inflicted upon the most innocent of children. Things are born only to decay or to be destroyed catastrophically.

Human perception and human reason tells us that we don't live in a realm of peace of any sort, not the Peace of Christ for sure, but also not any sort of lesser peace. For short times, we might enter a period of truce, but those periods don't last long. Those who know the stories of the earth and of men aren't fooled by mere lapses in violence.

Wolves and bears tear apart deer in their quest for food for themselves and their young. Men who can't or won't produce food or other necessary goods will arm themselves and kill or enslave others to get food, clothing, and shelter. Men will form large armies to swarm across the world conquering for the sake of power or massacring for the sake of hatred.

The earth itself isn't settled. Quakes can destroy cities of man. Volcanoes belch forth melted rock, in streams and in projectiles, to cover the cities of men or to set men and deer and trees aflame. Some eras have seen constant volcanic activity that covered vast plains with sheets of magma hundreds of yards deep. The final phases of melting by retreating glaciers have released great bodies of water. One such flood carved out parts of the Connecticut River Valley and passed on to slice a wide canal through Long Island. The plains of the Northwest of the United States show evidence of a still larger catastrophe of that same sort. Storms engulf or dissolve coastlands inhabited by millions of men and far more other animals. As recently as the 1890s, one of the last of the great storms of the Little Ice Age wiped out the Norwegian fishing fleets and coastal transportation fleets, killing thousands of tough, seagoing descendants of Vikings.

Nor are the heavens at peace, as some have imagined at times. Comets and asteroids have hit the earth often enough that geologists are still discovering vast craters on the Siberian plains or under the calm, warm waters of the Indian Ocean. Stars collide, sometimes producing explosions so powerful that they surprised even astronomers a few decades ago. Now astronomers can see far greater explosions as black holes form, perhaps by the collision of stars of unbelievable density, and those explosions can produce as much energy as entire galaxies, hundreds of billions of stars burning more quietly.

The Universe itself exploded out of an extremely dense state in an event called the Big Bang and often wrongly seen as some sort of a creation event. A billion years later, massive stars had formed as gas clouds collapsed. As the density approached no more than that of water on earth, those embryonic stars imploded to become nuclear fusion plants as repulsive forces between particles were overcome by gravity. Those stars were so massive that they quickly used up all their fuel and collapsed to an unstable state. Then they exploded, tossing heavier elements into the universe and it's these heavier elements which form the stuff of our bodies and our planet. Meanwhile, galaxies had started to form.

All of these processes continued and, on Earth, smaller scale violence had begun as crusts began to slide around on the surface of planets, leading to earthquakes, volcanoes, and other cataclysms. Before long, life was at work, organisms hunting and eating each other. Some lines of those lifeforms evolved to more complex forms by processes often involving violence. And more recently humans came upon the scene introducing higher intelligence deployed to the task of ripping open the earth or human bodies, killing Jews or Armenians or babies of all ethnic groups, exterminating entire species or destroying minds and souls for profit.

It's not a pretty picture when we concentrate on some of the details, but the universe is the physical foundation of a world, a story being told by God. Being a story, this world is morally ordered, ordered to the purposes of the Creator. We can't see those purposes clearly, though we've been told what they are.

We're told that the story moves toward the moment of Judgment, the

Apocalypse which is ever-present. It's not even a strictly chronological story as human stories must be. The climax and the ending of this story are not off in the future, to be found on the plains of Armageddon. The climax and the ending of this story have been with us and are being realized now and at each instant since the crucifixion of Jesus Christ. That climax and ending will be with us and will be realized at each and every instant that the mortal world exists. That climax and ending occur inside of each and every one of us as we live our lives, turning away from God or turning towards God.

And, so, I misspoke. In the midst of all this violence and chaos, there's peace and there are some who find it, being at peace even while the things swirl and melt around them, even while they feel they're drowning in the rapids of the modern world.

When we learn to sit quietly in the Presence of God, we can listen to Him. We can even start to make sense of the world,

There's both order and disorder in this world. Our efforts to make sense of this world, to see God's purposes in His story, can sometimes stretch us beyond our capabilities. And faith does not blind us, nor should it. The stronger our faith, the more we should feel the need to understand as much as we can. The stronger our faith, the more relentless should be our struggle to see in this world the purposes the Son of God revealed when He walked the earth and spoke with His fellow Israelites.

It might seem a contradiction at first but we also need to sit quietly, letting go of our anxieties and our fears that we might hear that whisper as did Elijah. The storms tear apart even rocks. The earthquakes reshape the land. The fires purge what's clean and filthy alike. And, after all these violent movements comes a quiet voice, a whisper. We should sit quietly in our caves, waiting for that whisper. Hearing it, we should emerge with feelings of great joy, prepared to worship our Maker.

> And [God] said [to Elijah], "Go forth, and stand upon the mount before the Lord." And behold, the Lord passed by, and a great and strong wind rent the mountains, and broke in pieces the rocks before the Lord, but the Lord was not in the wind; and after the wind an earthquake, but the Lord was not in the earthquake; and after the earthquake a fire, but the Lord was not in the fire; and after the fire a still small voice. And when Elijah heard it, he wrapped his face in his mantle and went out

> and stood at the entrance of the cave. [1 Kings 19:11-13a]

That still small voice was the voice of God and He speaks to each of us, offering the Peace of Christ for all who are brothers and sisters of Jesus Christ that we might share in His Life with the Father and the Holy Spirit.

## 1.2 The Human Battleground

We do not sin, we are sin. In more modern language:

> We are battlegrounds of order and disorder.

We're born in a largely disordered state and, if all goes well, we move to a state of order. We move to a state of perfect order by entering the Peace of Christ and we can do that only by allowing Christ to infuse His Being into our beings. This is the easiest and most personal way to see the gift God has offered us: He offers us His Son. He offered His Son on the cross to allow us to share divine life. He offers His Son as the groom to the Church and He offers His Son to each of us, to cleanse us and to fill us up and to perfect us. It doesn't often happen that any of us reach this state on this side of the grave, but it's our duty to persevere and to do what we can. We can only hope and pray that God will make up the difference.

But we typically move towards this Christlike state by stages, passing through various phases of animal order, sometimes passing through that noble state of a virtuous pagan. If order wins out to a substantial extent, a human being can take on the aspects of a person: unity, coherence, and completeness.

Mortal man is born with but one nature, that of a human animal. That nature is fragmented so that it would seem impossible that he can ever be unified to be but a single entity in any strong sense. For all the loose talk about human animals always being human persons, it's hard to imagine a mere animal of any species being able to take on the characteristics of a person. A fragmented man can be no person as such, no unified being; he's a collection of interacting biological and psychological processes and sometimes even some spiritual processes if he's seeking God.

To say that men are capable of becoming persons is the same as saying they are capable of entering the peace of Christ, capable of living with God, and that's possible only if men can receive a share of Christ's divinity. To say that a man is a true person is to say he has entered the peace of Christ, but that can't happen until his resurrection. On this side of the grave, we are all part of the world of development, of change, of decay.

## 1.3 A Delayed Battle – My Own Story

While I was just starting this book, I was dealing with a private disappointment that had caused me great pain and the feelings involved were quite intense. As often happens, I was barely detecting the healing touch of God. God was working, but He was working on His own schedule and not mine. Seven days and not a hint of healing. It had been a self-inflicted wound, but not so deep that I should have felt so much pain. But there were other disappointments in my life which had been with me for years and I was trying to summon up the strength and courage to move forward while I was reaping no benefits from past efforts.

I was starting several new writing projects and fearing the onset of financial problems. I was also sitting on top of a number of manuscripts, mostly novels, which had not been deemed worthy of publication. For fifteen years, I'd been writing serious books containing my deepest thoughts and feelings and I'd failed to publish a word. My heart and other parts of myself had begun to waver, to lose confidence even in my call from God. I'd realized that my writing vocation was, and is, a call from God, one perhaps leading up to my nonfiction books on Creation and on the spiritual lives appropriate to creatures, but I was losing faith in this realization. It hardly seemed worthwhile to sit down at the computer or the writing desk when completed works were simply filed away with seemingly no chance of ever being published.

On the whole, I wasn't feeling very good about my self or my place in the world of men. I'd been experiencing an ongoing conversion for more than 20 years and my life seemed somehow pointless. Whatever our need to make God first in our lives, we human beings are social creatures. We need to feel part of a human society. We desire to be respected but most will accept even the role of a despised member of a human society rather than living the life of a hermit. But I wished for respect. A saint I wasn't. I couldn't willingly accept the sort of abuse that many saints accepted.

And I found myself reviewing the past 20 years or so of my life. My conversion process was perhaps the dominant theme of those years, but

I was forced to admit, again, that I'd not really started writing for the purpose of serving God. My reasons were not evil by any means, but they were centered on my desires and not on God's desires for me – which I can only know imperfectly. My occasional dreams of fame and wealth had been secondary to the need to say something and to say something important, but that something had been my own thoughts and not thoughts which moved with the grain of God's Creation.

During my first years of writing, I'd found I hadn't much to say that was interesting but...

Some fragments of stories had been trying to come out. Individual scenes had been appearing in my mind but I'd not yet had enough experience to pull them together into coherent stories. There were two men hiking down a dirt road in northern New England. Thick were the forests on both side but stonewalls cut in and out without rhyme or reason to the sensibilities of the bigger man...

And there was the man who was under unbearable stress because he really didn't have the luck or the particular abilities to do well in his time and place. What could he do to develop that luck or those particular abilities? Oh, if only he could be a luckier man, a man of greater abilities, and yet be himself. Sort of.

Well, I went through years of struggle to figure out what those stories were and to tell them. Sort of.

Meanwhile, my conversion had changed me. Then again, when I tried to examine myself, nothing had changed. Not so far as I could tell.

Still, I'd begun to pray often and to sometimes pray deeply. After a nine-year interlude, I began to once again practice the Catholic faith I'd taken up near the beginning of my conversion. To my great surprise, I'd started to enjoy attending Mass. Not each and every Mass, but some. Then more. And then most. Nearly all.

It came to me that I was experiencing a little bit of life as God's companion. And then I had the strangest of thoughts:

> Suppose Heaven is a place that must be enjoyed on its own terms or else it would be... Hell?

In fact, I'd read that theologians had sometimes made a joke that Heaven and Hell were the same place. Because God's direct Presence would be all-encompassing, it would be Heaven only to those who truly loved God and Hell to all others.

Is Heaven a place of rewards for those who do good? Or is it, by gift of God, the true home of those who love their Maker?

Is Heaven a place where God plays the role of Walt Disney, working hard to please our passive selves? Or is it rather a place of continual worship and prayer? Is Heaven a place of Christian communion established for time without end?

If Heaven's a place of worship and prayer, then it must be that prayer and worship are the true ways of peace. It became clear to me that salvation was to be had only on God's terms, with His definition of what salvation is. We have no right and no power to demand that God meet our expectations about life in Heaven. He alone has the right and the power to decide our fates and He also knows better than us what's good for us. What's good for us is true life, the Life of Father and Son and Holy Spirit, and we have no more than hints of what that true life is like. Some of those hints come from the few seconds we're able to spend in the Peace of Christ.

By the time I'd started thinking along these lines, I knew enough history and enough sociobiology to realize that there are good reasons for men to have the characteristics which can lead so often to rebellion against their Maker or to simple acts of cruelty and greed against their fellowmen. The prophets and Jesus Himself confronted a stubborn nation, but stubbornness is a necessary characteristic for survival in tough lands, such as the Holy Land was during times of climatic stress or during times when the armies of gentiles were racing about looking for loot. Sexual lust? The major mistake of Darwin's successors, and Darwin himself at times, was to speak of natural selection when his theory made sense only as a theory of reproductive selection. The future belongs not to those who die with the most toys or the longest life or the largest body of slaves but rather to those who are members of family lines which make lots of babies who grow up to also be members of family lines which make lots of babies.

This isn't the place to speak of the false conflicts between modern science and Christianity. Still that false conflict often disturbs those who pay any attention to the National Geographic specials about our apish ancestors or the tales of quantum strangeness which appears in science fiction movies in the form of superstitions and magical events.

God is in charge and the world is such that our Maker has brought us to this point by means that can be explored by scientists and novelists, engineers and historians. Once there was a time when Christians could make sense of God's Creation by using ideas and images adopted from both the great pagan thinkers and also the pagan religions. That was good. Those ideas and views made sense in terms of the limited understanding of the empirical aspects of God's Creation. It was possible to build a limited understanding of God's Creation in its completeness and that limited understanding brought Christians some limited peace – they were able to make sense of the cosmos as being God's Creation. A well-educated man could be in the same state of peace as a simple believer for he knew that the teachings of the metaphysicians and mathematicians and astronomers made sense in light of the Apostle's Creed and the Bible.

We're the heirs of the ideas and images drawn from empirical reality by the Church Fathers and various Christian thinkers down through the centuries. But we now know that empirical reality isn't what Augustine thought, not what Luther or Bellarmine thought it to be. For that matter, it's not what Galileo or Newton thought it to be. Part of the unsettled feeling of the modern era comes from the apparent contradictions between modern empirical knowledge and our traditional views of physical reality. We often try to hold on to those traditional views of our world because they had been woven into various coherent stories which give some meaning to reality and to our lives within the context of revealed truths. Modern empirical knowledge hasn't yet been woven into any such story and this leads many people to imagine a conflict between science and Christianity. Be at peace on this issue, there can be no true conflict between God's work as a Creator of physical reality and the truths He revealed to us in more direct ways.

Our lack of a coherent understanding of the universe is part of the reason for those profound disturbances which have nurtured our moral and cultural decay. Mostly, we have failed to deal with the modern discovery that there's a universe and it's much like a story. It's not just a static setting for the story of the human race. When we see the stories which are physical reality, we get fresh understandings of the human story, even in its moral dimensions.

But I came to this line of thought by contemplating the damage done to modern men, including myself, by our ways of life. I tried to write novels to help myself and others to understand what had gone wrong. I did a lot of background reading in those days. I read in the fields of political philosophy and moral philosophy, history and political science, evolutionary biology and neurosciences, quantum mechanics and cosmological physics. I'd started reading serious novels for the first time since I was 15 or so.

Various pressures and fears forced me to write a book pulling together Christian revelation and modern empirical knowledge into one worldview. That book was *World*. After doing my best to understand the universe in light of Christian revelation, I found that my personal sources of distress remained. That is, I was a man who was still lonely – would I ever find friends who could share my interests? Would I ever find colleagues called to the same mission as myself? Or perhaps colleagues called to a different but compatible mission?

And so that returns me to the great disappointment. I'd gotten too excited and too hopeful about a very tentative romantic friendship, likely just because I was, and still am, unwilling to adapt myself to this society we created; thus, I was looking for my own haven of sorts. The euphoria of my first book being published had led me to the delusion that my life would settle down and become more pleasant in all areas. On my schedule – right now. But some good had come of my loss of control. Barriers in my inner self had broken down. Unity was a clearer possibility though my pain hid that insight from me for a while.

## The One Standard of Perfection

Medieval theologians and philosophers spoke of God as being 'simple'. Why would they say such a thing? The full answer's a bit complex and would take some contemplation to understand. I'll try to simplify matters a bit. They were using the creaturely concept of 'simple' analogically to summarize the insight:

> God has no parts in the way of a creature, no organs and no limbs. He doesn't change or decay in the way of a creature.

Because we're heirs to those thinkers, we assume much of what they fought to understand. But their efforts to understand God resulted in analogies and images that were appropriate for their times and for their understanding of Creation and also appropriate for the particular errors they were struggling against. They're no longer appropriate and have turned into superstitions in some cases, but not because they were irrational. Ideas become irrational if held when they no longer make sense given what we know of God's Creation and God's Word.

Before I go on, I'll answer a question which may be arising in the minds of attentive readers:

> Am I preaching a doctrine in which truths change according to the spirit of the times?

No. Absolutely not. In fact, the opposite is true and that created a weird sort of unrest in my soul. Early on in my career as an amateur theologian, I decided to take seriously the warnings of Sacred Scripture and of great Christian thinkers: even the absolute truths of God's revelations must be stated in terms of human words, of analogies and images drawn from the Creation which is a tiny, tiny reflection of God's greatness. Seen in that way, theologians and philosophers, poets and scientists, even the Evangelists and St. Paul, are blind men trying to figure out the nature of the elephant.

There are those who were made by God so that they need a lot of stability, and these become legalistic. The Pharisees will always be with us. They fought St. Augustine, St. Thomas Aquinas, and the Fathers of the Council of Trent, but soon enough had taken over and distorted the works of all of these into rigid, lifeless views of the living God and His living Creation. Moses received the original self-revelations of God as an image of a living bush which was aflame, burning without ever diminishing its substance, without ever burning out. Certainly, the Ten Commandments are important but Jews and Christians alike might ask themselves: If I am a truly God-centered human being, why do I not follow such laws naturally out of love of the living God? For that God, the living God, the true God can be represented as a burning bush but not a stone tablet.

Truly do we need laws and rigorous moral codes to train ourselves. We're not the strong and insightful creatures we imagine ourselves to be, nor do our conscious parts have so great a control over our other parts as we would imagine. We discipline all our parts by developing proper habits and not just by learning rules and trying to apply them as the need arises. We'll fail to become morally well-ordered creatures if we pretend we can ignore the needs and powers of those silent parts of our own beings.

In any case, all of us should be moving towards the state where we do what's right out of love for God and for God's Creation. This is a precondition of the Peace of Christ. Jesus taught us we can become perfect.

He commanded us to be perfect as our Father is perfect, though Jesus didn't promise we could actually reach that state on this side of the grave.

To be perfect and to live in the Peace of Christ are one and the same for a human being. In simpler terms, we can be perfect only by being at peace, with our own selves and with Creation and with our Creator. This is most certainly easier said than done.

## 1.4 What is the Peace of Christ?

Before speaking more of the Peace of Christ, I'll speak of God. If we're to join God in His life of peace, we should have some understanding of who God is. I'll take the viewpoint of St. Thomas Aquinas who considered God to be His own Act-of-being. Though three Persons, God is One, and He's more specifically One Supreme Act-of-being.

The Peace of Christ is the Quiet and the Stillness of that explosion of energy, absolutely infinite in His own Act-of-being in a way that is beyond the words and concepts of mathematics and metaphysics. The Peace of Christ is that divine calm infused into those men who turn themselves over to Christ, who eat of His Body and drink of His Blood, allowing the stuff of He who is true God and true man to permeate their own being. By doing so, a mortal man can begin to share in this divine being, this simplicity and peace which is infinitely energetic even as it's also absolutely calm.

There is but one God, though He be three Persons. There is but one Peace, the Peace which is the love binding Father and Son and Holy Spirit. When I say the Peace of Christ, I mean that same love offered to men that they might share in the life of God, might become companions of God for time without end. The Peace of Christ is what binds our own insides, giving the unity and coherence and completeness which are the attributes of both a world and a person, as I discussed in *World*.

We cannot be persons by our own strength, nor on our own merits, for a person is an entity that corresponds to the one standard of perfection which is the Peace of Christ, the Peace that surpasses all understanding. We can be persons only by allowing Christ to fill us so that we can enter the realm of divine peace hand in hand with our Lord Jesus Christ, children holding the hand of their older Brother as they return to the Father of Christ and the Father of Christ's brothers and sisters.

## How Could Jesus Bring Us into Divine Love?

How could a creature, a man, bring us into a realm which is ordered and unified by divine love? Even if we believe that Jesus was the Christ, the human nature of the Son of God, He was also a man living on Earth. He was a finite man, found inside of one human skin, having lived a particular life amongst a particular people speaking a particular language and having a particular understanding of God's Creation.

The simple answer is that Jesus of Nazareth is the human nature of the divine Person we Christians call the Son of God. This is the way in which a Thomistic existentialist might state the basic beliefs of the Christian tradition:

- God is three Persons in one supreme Act-of-being. God is His own Act-of-being. The three Persons are Father, Son, and Holy Spirit.
- Jesus Christ, the Son of God, has two natures, human and divine, in His one Person.
- Jesus of Nazareth is the human nature of the divine Person we Christians call the Son of God.

Jesus Christ is God, the Person of the Son of God. He's truly God, God from God. He is also truly man, conceived by the power of the Holy Spirit in the womb of Mary. Along with the Father and the Holy Spirit, Jesus is our Creator, the Creator of all that exists that's not God. As St. Augustine realized, our Creator is more deeply inside of us than we are ourselves. It's our Creator Who binds our insides, Who brings us into rational order, Who completes us so that we can become true persons.

As Christ infuses His own Person into our human beings, the process begins of binding our anxious, confused selves into human persons capable of living in the Peace of Christ. There's little we can do to consciously guide the process along by ourselves though a good spiritual guide might well be God's good servant in helping us to gain true unity and true coherence and true completeness in our human beings. More likely it is in this disordered world that a human being moves towards the Peace of Christ by a painful process guided by the Almighty Who's not always concerned about our comfort or safety or prosperity during our mortal lives. He's more concerned about our salvation and also the role we play in His story – including the effect we can have on others who can be turned to God or others who are already trying to work their ways towards salvation.

Only God can bring creatures such as ourselves to a state where we can live again after death. He might use human beings and human institutions as His instruments and He saves us into the Body of Christ – the Church. Yet it's God and God alone who can take what we are and make of us creatures who are capable of living as His companions for time without end – without that true life turning into a hellish existence. If we were to remain the fragmented creatures we are in our mortal lives, we would become too aware of the gaps and broken regions in our innermost selves. We would remain Dr. Jekylls, with Heavenly external behaviors and hellish insides.

At various times, some of us wonder:

> Why did God not save all of us without putting us through this misery? Why did the Lord not make all of us persons able to share His life? Why did our Creator make us fragmented creatures struggling towards coherence in our thoughts and our very beings, creatures who can only dream of being complete? If He's in the deepest parts of our being, why did He not pull us together into Christ-like beings, true persons, from our very conceptions?

The answer I gave in *World* is pretty straightforward. God is telling a particular story in which the human race has come into existence over billions of years by processes which sometimes seem rather grotesque and brutal. In this story, individual human beings develop during lives that often involve much pain and suffering. God has chosen freely to tell this tale, a tale in which there's evil and suffering, a tale in which His Son is incarnated a man, suffers, dies, and is buried that He might become the first of the resurrected. And we must remember this:

> We're part of this story, part of this particular world God shaped from Creation. If God had created a better world with better creatures, that world wouldn't have been ours and those creatures wouldn't have been us.

God told us He loved us before the world began. He chose to love us in a special way rather than choosing to love some of the infinity of other creatures who could have come into existence. Why didn't He create all possible creatures? God chose to love us in that special way, an active way. We came to be as a result of the Almighty's choice.

So, I return to the question:

> Why did God not save all of us without putting us through this misery? Why did the Lord not make all of us persons able to share His life? Why did our Creator make us fragmented creatures struggling towards coherence in our thoughts and our very beings, creatures who can only dream of being complete? If He's at the deepest parts of our being, why did He not pull us together into Christ-like beings, true persons, from our very conceptions?

It's proper to question what God has done, proper to ponder why we are what we are, why our world is what it is. In the end, this world is more a story than a setting for autonomous beings who could have been set down in any old world. We should ask the questions proper to a story and its characters rather than thinking of ourselves as autonomous individuals who could have been in a different and better world.

Perhaps there's a certain richness to our being that'll come from our living through this sort of suffering and death? Perhaps that richness pleases our Maker? I don't know. Maybe God could have told this story so that there was less pain and suffering but that's His business. We should try to be at peace on the issue of evil knowing that our Father knows what's best for us. He wishes to save us and He's offering us a path to Heaven.

## Fostering Fragmentation

We're fragmented creatures, having little more than hints of the unity, coherence, and completeness that would be personhood. We modern people are willfully nurturing our fragmentation because we're thus able to satisfy desires of some of our components. And we have components we favor over others – let there be no doubt that there are conflicts between our various parts in our current state.

For example, our sexuality, can easily conflict with our more recently evolved component of abstract, self-aware brain activity that we usually call 'reason'. Our higher-level moral awareness can often be in active conflict with our raw desires to reproduce. But the problem has been intensified in the modern world, and perhaps in some earlier complex civilizations, in that our fragmentation is encouraged to the advantage of certain Principalities and Powers. For example, corporate entities such as centralized governments or commercial corporations will act to destroy our bonds to families and local communities, including communities of worship, just because those earthly Principalities and Powers act as if to absorb us, all of us. We're small creatures and we have only limited hours in the day to serve those to whom we feel loyalty, and worldly institutions need all of our available hours that we might work and consume to their benefit. They're jealous gods indeed.

We have formed new bonds, to various gods of the marketplaces. We're dependent upon corporate executives in Chicago or Taipei for our jobs, and they're dependent upon financiers in London or Singapore for the credits to expand that plant or distribution center. We depend upon Congress and the bureaucrats of the Social Security Administration or the international insurance industry for our medical benefits and our retirement benefits.

It's an unhealthy situation for human animals, as well as being a situation in which God and communities which worship God are squeezed out. We pretend to have some sort of spiritual aspects which allow us to remain centered on family or church, even as we devote our greater energies to the gods of the marketplaces, even as we encourage our more talented youth to serve those gods and not the God of Jesus Christ.

And we feel ourselves justified in our rebellions against our own biological natures as well as against God. We're weary and we're frightened. We seek a safe harbor where we can rest. We seek assurances that our pains will be eased and that we'll not suffer hunger, nor bone-deep exhaustion, nor sleeplessness. Over the past two centuries, the gods of the marketplaces, political and commercial, have been remarkably successful at taking care of our material needs. They've been far more successful at this task than the God of Jacob and Israel ever was, but He didn't seem to make our comfort and safety His highest priority. And this is not the first showing of the great might of the gods of the marketplaces. For all the efforts of the scribes who wrote Chronicles to whitewash King Solomon, the more honest 1 Kings shows him as so corrupted that he was willing to sell part of the Promised Land to obtain building materials. We must remember he was building pagan temples for his wives as well as the so-called Temple of Solomon. He enslaved many of his fellow Israelites, directly or by way of oppressive taxes, but those who prospered lived well indeed.

Economic prosperity is often far less God-centered than it first appears and sometimes is limited to a small percentage of the population. And it brings war and restless activity far more often than it brings peace and security.

God did not promise "Peace on earth, goodwill for men." The better translators tell us the angels said "Peace on earth for men of goodwill." This is not a promise of worldly peace, but rather a foretelling of the peace possible for Christ-centered men even in the midst of persecutions and wars and plagues and famines.

We can see the distortion of God's message show up in the corruption of American Christianity over the period of prosperity, a corruption that is seen in the enthusiastic Christian reception of Xmas hymns, Dickens' "Christmas Carol" oddly empty of Christ, and, most sadly, in the determination of so many Catholic bishops and Protestant leaders to merge their flocks in with the flocks that worship not Jesus but Abraham Lincoln, not the God who sent John the Baptist into the wilderness but rather the gods of the marketplaces who draw us out of our families and local communities, including our church communities.

We don't really like the world as we receive it from God. We'll do our best to reshape our own bodies and our social relationships, rather than doing our best to lead lives serving God and our fellowmen. We do with our technology what satisfies the desires of men rather than what's right according to the Word of God.

Can peace be had? Not in the vast marketplaces of the modern world. They give us an array of houses, catalogs of laborsaving devices, and an extraordinary choice of entertainment. The houses draw us away from the natural communities of our youth. The laborsaving devices must be earned by long workweeks in the inhuman cubicles of the modern workplaces. The entertainment turns us into passive, exploitable carbon-based entities.

We give up what's human, what's potentially Christ-like, when we allow the gods of the marketplaces to shape us. We also give up any chance for a true peace. We get at best a truce with the world, a truce that breaks down as soon as troubles show up. And troubles will show up. By an accident of peace, Americans had few troubles during the 20th century. We were prosperous and didn't suffer badly even during the great wars of that bloody century. When the traditional Asian powers were slowly rising from their centuries of political trouble aggravated by colonial exploitation, when the European powers were dealing with the mass graves and cities turned to rubble after their attempts to commit continental suicide, the United States was pretty much intact.

We mistook luck for the blessings of God and we saw this American Oasis in the bloody modern era as a period and a region of true peace. We set out to establish a man-centered peace and this involved the building of vast armament factories, the training of the largest deployable military force in history, and the reconstruction of our society to the needs of the gods of the marketplaces, no different from the Principalities and Powers of St. Paul.

We have dismantled what was truly human, what had God-centered potential, and have used the pieces to build places belonging to the gods of the marketplaces and not to us. The Peace of Christ is not the peace of a prosperous middle-class society, though that lesser peace can be very good in itself. But that lesser peace can also be allied to a willful ignorance of crimes being committed to sustain it. There have been prosperous societies which were morally well-structured by human standards. Again – that's not bad. But even the development of a truly moral human society shouldn't let us fool ourselves into believing we've achieved the deeper and truer peace which only God can give us. And we should remember that human beings not yet infused with Christ cannot handle peace very well. We get complacent and begin to think of that peace as being our own doing. And we overestimate that peace, mistaking an oasis for the Holy Land.

In fact, we're finite creatures with finite attention spans and finite tolerance for any activity – no matter how pleasurable or how interesting. The true miracle of resurrection is not God raising us from the dead – that's no more amazing than His acts of bringing us into existence during our mortal lives. The true miracle of resurrection is that we'll remain us and yet be capable of enjoying the Peace of Christ, capable of being His companions for time without end.

Our fragmentation will be at an end. We'll be able to concentrate on the important things, enjoying them for time without end.

In the meantime, we often nurture the fragmentation which can be useful for protecting ourselves from painful healing processes. The path to the Peace of Christ travels through regions of healing and pain. The very process of converting a human animal into a human person will typically involve certain types of pain as the the great spiritual masters have told us – such as St. Theresa of Avila and St. John of the Cross.

But that process is necessary for the reason I stated above: in our present state, we wouldn't be happy as God's companions for time without end. We might enjoy a few centuries. Then we'd spend a few millenia wishing someone would build a cable television system. Then we would spend time without end wishing it would end.

# 2 Visiting the Realm of Peace

Already being a God-centered man – however defectively and incompletely, I suffered my disappointment and dealt with my personal problem by visiting the best therapist possible two or three times a day. I was going to silently pray in front of the tabernacle in which the Body of Christ rested. For those who aren't Catholics, the Body of Christ in the tabernacle is the Blessed Sacrament, the bread which has been consecrated by God, changed into the Body of His Son, in response to the Eucharistic prayers and invocations of a true Christian priest.

> So Jesus said to them, "Truly, truly, I say to you, unless you eat the flesh of the Son of man and drink his blood, you have no life in you; he who eats my flesh and drinks my blood has eternal life, and I will raise him up at the last day. For my flesh is food indeed, and my blood is drink indeed. He who eats my flesh and drinks my blood abides in me, and I in him. As the living Father sent me, and I live because of the Father, so he who eats me will live because of me. This is the bread which came down from heaven, not such as the fathers ate and died for he who eats this bread will live forever." [John 6:53-58]

I long for peace and one way for me to achieve peace is to prepare myself by studying, contemplating, and writing what comes to me as I try to align my thoughts with those which God wishes me to have. But there are other ways that must be traveled at the same time, and some of those other ways are of the utmost importance. Some of those ways are ways of faith, the faith which must precede true understanding, including a true understanding of the physical universe.

So, I was visiting Christ two or three times a day in addition to going to daily Mass. At Mass, I was able to chew and swallow the very Body of Christ that He might fill me up. I knew I couldn't become Christ-like, I couldn't enter the realm of true Peace, by my own efforts. I couldn't ascend to God. In fact, there's no place to climb towards. I was beginning to realize that I must live the life God was giving me and pray that God's grace will complete and perfect my human animal nature, making of my a suitable companion for His Son, our Lord Jesus Christ.

In addition to receiving Jesus at Mass, it's good for us to spend some time sitting quietly in front of the Blessed Sacrament, just listening if He might choose to speak in some way, but mostly just offering ourselves to the Lord as a friend and companion. To be near the Blessed Sacrament brings a Christian nearer to God in a way that's hard to describe. There are times to give God praise, times to thank Him for blessings, and times to ask Him for help. But we should spend part of our prayer time sitting quietly in front of God. Sometimes, we'll just feel alone and restless, but sometimes we'll feel the Presence of God in a special way. The dry and boring times are as important as the fruitful times. As a great runner once said: we win races during those practices when we don't want to be there and nothing seems to be going right.

Our relationship to God is that of creature to Creator and He's a Creator who's yet in our deepest parts, bringing us into being and shaping us. As we mature spiritually, we should be learning not to reach out to Him but rather to let Him complete and perfect our human natures. We should be learning to think along with God, to speak along with God, to listen along with God, to act along with God. An impossible goal in this lifetime, perhaps, but the very recognition of our duty to our Maker will let us understand why St. Augustine claimed that the man who truly loves God can do as he wishes. That man who truly loves God wishes what God wishes.

On a quiet, gray Sunday in early October, I went for a walk an hour or so after attending the early Mass. I wandered for 30 minutes and then arrived at St. John the Baptist after the second morning Mass. I was a mess inside though not nearly so bad a mess as I'd been after personal crises in previous years. And I knelt there, praying first the Jesus Prayer:

> Lord Jesus Christ, Son of the living God, have mercy on me, a sinner.

And then I offered up another short prayer:

> Your will be done, Lord, not mine. In Your time, Lord, not mine.

And then I sat there feeling hurt and bitter. I was in an evil mood though I was struggling hard to control that evil mood and I was succeeding to some extent by human standards. Inside my head were thoughts of moving to another part of the country, of finding a new community of people who would appreciate me. I even thought of moving to an isolated region and becoming a hermit of sorts. Unlike prior crises, even some a few short years before, I didn't think of turning from God or His Church.

And I repeated the Jesus Prayer and then my prayer of submission to God. And then I prayed once more:

> Your will be done, Lord, not mine. In Your time, Lord, not mine.

I was begging that God burn out of me that which was not proper, that which had led me to improper feelings and then had led me into a state of deep bitterness. I was praying for the grace of submission to God's will, for the grace of living by His schedule.

And suddenly I felt not alone. My Lord was present inside of me, as He had been when I was feeling so bad, as He always had been and will be so long as I exist. But I was suddenly aware of His presence and my willfulness broke down.

I had submitted to the true God, the God of Jesus Christ, and my childish and self-centered will had dissolved. I had no will as such but I had myself and that self was a bit more unified. I was focused upon the God who was present more deeply in myself than I could be. That act of focusing upon God was itself beyond my powers and had surely come as a gift from God at a time when it was needed.

The Peace of Christ had come upon me as a result of my submission to God. And it would disappear often over the succeeding weeks and months, will likely disappear often to the end of my mortal life.

> Your will be done, Lord, not mine. In Your time, Lord, not mine.

The tears were running down my cheek. My will was broken. And I felt healthier and more unified in my being than I'd ever felt. In the next few days, I would continue to live in the Peace of Christ, walking around in a fog of sorts, as if I were in love once more. In this life, in our mortal experiences, the Peace of Christ is, in fact, much like a mortal love. It'll not continue unbroken. This is not due to any defects in the Peace of Christ but rather to the sinful and frail nature of our natural beings.

In this life, we'll never be able to fully let down our barriers to God, and we'll never have more than brief moments when we can think with Him, feel with Him, act with Him. We'll usually try, and fail, to perceive Him as we perceive a human companion – outside of us and sitting on that chair on the opposite side of the table. And, yet, one day we'll be face-to-face with Jesus Christ, true God and true man.

# 3 Peace as Salvation

## 3.1 What is Salvation?

The world can be described as a struggle between order and disorder. As creatures in this world, we human beings can also be described as entities which are warriors and battleground alike in a war between order and disorder. Salvation must certainly mean an end to these violent struggles, those inside of us as well as those outside of us. Surely, salvation consists of the establishment of a just order, not an order of ongoing trial.

That just order isn't a new gift from God so much as it's a completion and perfection of the social order appropriate to a species of apes – *homo sapiens* or the human race. There are those who imagine the world of the resurrected to be a totally different sort of world than this valley of tears, but we should prefer to see that better world as a better version of this world. As some Medieval scholastics claimed: grace doesn't destroy nature or replace nature; grace completes and perfects nature. This world is a type of the world to come, but that world will not contain death or any of the related states of decay or chaos. We'll have a share of God's own life but mediated through Jesus Christ, God's Son in perfected human flesh.

We're social creatures, living in various sorts of relationships with those in our families and local communities, also those who are aliens to us. Most of the modern ideologies deny this aspect of our being, claiming we're individuals who gather together in ways that do not change our individualistic nature. A modern man is told he's essentially an autonomous agent, selecting a lifestyle in the same way he selects a toothpaste. In fact, he tries to select a lifestyle by shopping around for consumer goods that satisfy his needs and desires, a spouse who excites his passions, a worship community that affirms him in his various choices. In acting this way, he'll give up the limited freedom proper to a human being – he'll become a thing to be exploited by the those hungry for wealth or power.

Such a wretched being is likely to seek momentary pleasures over the possibility of peace without end. After all, that true peace, the Peace of Christ, is a gift from God given to those He chooses and given at a time of His choosing. The Lord Almighty knows what's good for His chosen ones and He isn't about to conduct a market survey to find out what we think we need to be happy for time without end.

We modern human beings minimize our social ties that we might move about more freely in the marketplaces, and few nowadays understand those social ties and how they're more a part of our being than the more obvious parts of ourselves. Relationships exist first, even before matter. God didn't create the world in the way of a watchmaker. The Almighty didn't need a thing present for Him to love it. He chose to love and the world came to be as a direct result of His holy desire to see it and to watch it unfold. Only God can literally create something from nothing by loving it, but we also shape and are shaped by relationships. And we shape others by forming appropriate relationships with them.

When we raise children, we guide them and try to form their basic moral characters at an early age. We try to encourage the development of their moral reasoning during their years of adolescence and early adulthood. Those children and young adults have traits which can develop into virtues or vices. There are not some who have the virtues of sexual love which lead to stable marriages and good families and others who have the vices of sexual hunger which lead to promiscuous behavior and perhaps serial polygamy. We have sexual desires, driving forces for the reproductive needs of our genetic lines – the human race and the more particular families we belong to. Those desires are the expression of a sexual nature which can turn towards stable and respectful love of a human being from the opposite sex. Or those desires can be given up to better serve God and His Church. Or they can turn to lust. The final shape of these human traits is determined by the relationships of that developing human being and the way he responds to the relationships which others form with him or offer to him.

We human beings are creatures with intentional desires and some of the desires of each of us have undoubtedly been turned towards virtue and others towards vice. Whatever our particular situation or the situations of those around us, we should let ourselves be aware of the Presence of God and let Him place our feet upon the path to salvation. Always remember that love will overcome a multitude of sins, but also remember that we often have trouble feeling love, for God or our neighbor or even our own selves. When we feel no love, when we feel dry inside, we should stay the course – continue to pray, to read the Bible, to worship God. Most of all, we should do what we can to think and feel along with God that we may also start loving along with God.

Remember also that we're still children in God's eyes, though we can be spiteful little beasts at times. He's a Father who chastises most harshly those He loves the best, but He does this to suit His purposes. One of those purposes is the nurturing and disciplining of potential companions for His Son. We shouldn't overestimate our importance in the general scheme of things and we shouldn't think in self-centered ways, but we must have faith that our good is served by God's greater purposes.

God made the universe as a whole. We're part of this universe, and the true miracle of salvation is that God will somehow help us to become creatures suitable to be companions to His Son for time without end. The miracle is that we can become holy enough that the Holy Spirit might be at home inside us, binding us to the Father and the Son.

And this is salvation: to enjoy true life for time without end. The only way for that to happen is for us to become companions of Jesus Christ, for us to share the very life of God.

God became man that men might share the Life of God.

## 3.2 What is Saved?

A strange way to phrase the question when I'm dealing with the salvation of human beings. Should I not be saying, "Who is saved?". I don't know for sure but I think the proper question really and truly is, "What is saved?" just because we're not born as persons in a Christian sense and we're not purely individuals.

That is, our being is fully contained within the context of our relationship with our Creator. I'm not talking about a conscious relationship. It's God who chose to love us and few of us are aware of that love in a truly conscious way. When we become aware of God's personal love for us, we're starting to enter the Peace of Christ and that will happen at a time of God's choosing.

The universe itself is no more, and no less, than an object of God's love. God chose to love the universe and the universe came into existence. God chose to love us and we came into existence. God made us because He chose to actively love us before we came to be, but that chosen relationship of loving us is not separate from His role as Creator. Nor is His act of loving us different from His act of creating us.

> What God loves actively, He creates. What He creates, He loves actively. The two actions are but one, and they are acts-of-being.

The very substance of our bodies comes from God's act of love. And, so, the first part of the answer to, "What is saved?" is simply, "God's relationship to a human being He loves." We aren't so important as we might think even when it comes to us.

We shouldn't think of the world as existing independent of God, a place He visits on occasion. Nor should we think of anything as existing independent of God. Not an atom, not a speck of space nor an instant of time, exists unless God brings it into existence on an ongoing basis. God is here, inside of us, inside of each moment of time, each speck of matter or seemingly empty space. We aren't aware of His Presence without His help because we perceive substances, stuff. We also perceive relationships between things made of stuff. We don't perceive existence in itself and God is a pure Act-of-being, I-am. God doesn't need stuff and has nothing corresponding to a body, except for the human body His Son took up to Himself as a second nature.

Human beings are made by God though He has used complex, evolutionary processes we don't always approve of. Not being divine, human beings are made of substance. God created that substance, the chemicals of our bodies, as an act of love – He loved the world before it existed. He created us as living beings as acts of love which show themselves as a shaping of human nature over billions of years of evolution and then a shaping of each of us as individuals over our lifetimes. Our human selves aren't independent of the loves and dependencies and habits we engage in during our mortal lives. We're not independent of the loves gifted upon us by God and man and golden retriever. I pray that my parents are with the Lord Jesus Christ and that means that I'm praying their love for me and my love for them is part of that world of the Resurrected.

What is saved? Not the substance of our earthly bodies for sure, though we'll have perfected bodies like that of the Resurrected Christ. Yet, it's closer to the truth to say that our bodily natures are saved than to speak of our souls being saved, so long as we think of souls as being something different from our mortal selves. St. Thomas Aquinas had a very limited idea of a soul as a non-human entity attached to us that we might be able to engage in abstract thought. If he had known how dynamic matter is, how it's made of the same underlying stuff as energy and fields, he would have probably given up any idea of a soul. Still, he understood our bodily natures well enough to see our virtues, even our loves, are founded in our bodies. Thus, he could claim:

> My soul [in Thomas the organ for thought] is not I; and if only souls are saved, I am not saved, nor is any man. [From the *Commentary to 1 Corinthians 15* by St. Thomas Aquinas as quoted by Hannah Arendt in *The Life of the Mind* (page 43)]

Our bodies are objects of God's love. We need no greater glory than this and have no possibility of greater glory than to be loved by God. God's love for us is already perfect, but we can't often feel it directly because we need to develop our human faculties to a higher state, a Christ-like state, before we can feel that divine love. If we could feel God's love in our mortal lives, we wouldn't have to search for the Peace of Christ. We would be living in it, because it's the same love which binds Father, Son, and Holy Spirit. It's that love which will bring our resurrected selves into a true companionship with Jesus Christ and His Father and Their Spirit. And it's that love which created us and continues to create us each instant of our lives.

Love is what we take with us, but even that's not quite right. For it's love that brings us out of the grave. What's saved is a human being as object of the particular love God feels for that man or woman or child.

Even the Incarnate Son of God struggled at times in this life as He dealt with the Cross He could see clearly during His mortal life. Even He prayed to the Father for strength, as He struggled with the weakness which is part of this mortal life. It's not a sinful life in a fallen world. It's a life in which God is helping His chosen to move towards their destiny as friends of His Son.

However we describe our basic human nature, we know that we don't feel the love of God directly. We can't even be sure that God exists since we can't perceive the God who is pure existence, I-am. We can't be sure that He's here with us as we struggle, as we head towards our deaths. We can protest we're sure, and we are often right to bluff, telling ourselves that our faith will never fail. But it can fail just because we see what's most important as through a glass darkly.

For reasons we don't understand fully, we aren't born with well-developed faculties to perceive He Who truly exists. After all, we evolved in a world of substance and our organs of perception and even our higher organs of conception are suited for dealing with entities of creaturely substance and also with the relationships between those entities. Those entities exist as objects of God's love but we see the volcano or the little girl and not the love which brings them into existence and shapes them. And, yet, our minds and hearts can be disciplined by praying and reading the Bible and worshiping so that we can realize that God is present each thing that exists – else it would cease to exist. Even those in the advanced stages of conversion can have great trouble in perceiving God's Presence, in feeling His love. St. Teresa went through years of dryness when she couldn't feel a hint of divine love and Blessed Mother Teresa of Calcutta was in a similar state for most of her adult life.

We can speculate on the reasons that many, including great saints, have trouble being aware of the Presence of God, but this isn't a place for philosophical or theological discussions. It's a place to note that we're brought into being by God's love. We're shaped by His love and by the love of others around us.

It's these relationships of love which will be saved. It's these relationships of love, especially the love God gives to us, that will raise us from the grave into the blessed realm where we can live for time without end as companions to Jesus Christ. It's these relationships of love which will bring our resurrected bodies into existence.

The body of the Resurrected Christ was more perfect than His mortal body. This isn't because of a magical change of bodies. He didn't have a human soul that separated from His mortal body and somehow attached itself to a perfected body. That body was part of a risen man, one who was also the Son of God. That body was more perfect because it was the object of a more direct love. The perfected human body of Jesus was united more directly to the Father and the Holy Spirit. The Son of God had returned to His Father and Their Spirit after He had completed the processes of biological and social development, having learned obedience.

When it was finished, when Jesus had died on the cross and He had given up His mortal life to His Father, He was ready to return to the Father and their Spirit. There was no longer a need for the Father to shield His presence or His love in any way.

It'll be the same with us in important ways. What's saved is God's love for us whereas Jesus was Himself God. But we'll receive a gift that will make us true brethren of Christ. If we're deemed worthy of participating in the resurrection, then God's love will be more direct. With such a love, the object of love, us, will be perfected to the extent possible. We'll still be finite creatures, objects of divine Love rather than being ourselves sources of divine Love. At that, we'll be able to share that divine Love with all those others in the Body of Christ.

## 3.3 Where Will We Be Saved?

We'll be saved in a world which is energized more directly by the love of God. There will be no more need for shade or shadows, for the story which produces companions for the Son of God will be ended and they will live in a new story as companions to God.

But where is this place in terms we can grasp. Is it above us, on the other side of the moon's orbit? There's a lot out there beyond the moon. The universe seems to contain at least 100 billion galaxies, each holding 100 billion stars or more. Until the vast expansion of empirical knowledge in the past few centuries, human beings had thought that Heaven, the divine realm, was out there beyond the orbit of the moon. No such realm shows up in our star maps and boys and girls sit in front of the television sets in their parlors watching as starships fly through regions empty of angels and seemingly empty of God.

We should recognize the unsettling effect of empirical knowledge that's in conflict with the knowledge used in past centuries to understand God's Creation. We now know that there is no Heaven on the other side of the moon's orbit and no Hell miles below our feet. Does this mean that Heaven and Hell don't exist? That's a more confusing and confused question than we might believe. All we need to know is that we live in God's Creation. Facts being discovered by scientists, well-grounded theories proposed by scientists, deal with God's Creation. If we have our faith, then we – far more than scientistic skeptics – can move forward to embrace these facts and theories that we might better understand God's Creation. We shouldn't fear that this new scientific knowledge has cast any doubts on the Christian claim that God has promised to save at least some of us, to bring us to a life without end, a life in which there will be no strife or pain or suffering.

It's the promise that grounds our belief and not any inherited human speculations, not even those which were made by great saints. That promise didn't depend upon spatial relationships between Heaven and Hell and Earth – Heaven was promised to those destined to be God's friends and that's what we know for sure. That's all we need to know to go on with our efforts to center our lives on God.

The details of the possible relationships between earth and Heaven have changed but such possibilities have always been human speculations and always will be on this side of the grave. God promised to save those who belong to the Lord Jesus Christ and such a promise remains intact to believers, unlikely to skeptics, impossible to unbelievers on an earth shooting along with the Milky Way at tens of thousands of miles per hour. It remains the same in a universe in which 100 billion galaxies were once packed into a space smaller than a typical atom under present conditions.

Maybe I can describe a way of viewing Heaven and this universe as being part of the same Creation. This sort of view might allow us a little bit more peace and confidence the next time someone starts talking about modern science being opposed to Christian ideas.

First of all, we need to realize that the so-called Big Bang is not a moment of Creation. It couldn't be. We can see it, at least through the imaginations of cosmological physicists working with vast arrays of data collected by astronomical instruments. We couldn't see a Creation event, not the real one. We couldn't see that because we can't see nothing and we wouldn't be able to see something emerging from nothing. We can't even imagine it because we can't truly imagine nothing.

The Big Bang is the beginning of an expansion of this universe from extremely dense conditions. We really can't yet describe the dense conditions back beyond a certain time. The best of theories proposed by 2007 describe events only a small fraction of a second after the expansion began. Conditions were so extreme that the very properties of the universe were changing rapidly. The universe was going through a variety of phase changes, analogical to the phase changes that water goes through when it freezes and becomes ice or boils and starts turning to a vapor, a gas. The underlying stuff is the same but human beings know that ice and water have that same underlying stuff only because of observations of ice melting to become water and water freezing to become ice.

The early stages of the universe, those small fractions of a second after the beginning of the expansion, were what they were and we can only come to understand such aspects of God's Creation by observing nature in a disciplined way and then putting together some sort of a story of those events by way of a disciplined imaginative effort. Mathematics can be used to nearly miraculous effect in helping us to understand but we need the observations which come various relics of that early expansion, such as the so-called microwave background radiation – which actually came from a time hundreds of thousands of years after the expansion which we call the Big Bang started. As yet, scientists can't see back past the later time when the microwave background radiation was generated except in the imaginative use of mathematics but some of the resulting theories are very convincing and largely supported by high-energy experiments on earth.

What results from all this mathematics and experimentation and astronomical observation is a narrative set inside of a Christian faith that God exists, that He's all-powerful and all-good, and that He created all that is not Himself. In *World*, I traveled backward in time through this narrative, reaching the so-called Big Bang and then traveled past that in a very speculative way, though I subjected my thought to the disciplines of modern mathematics, modern physics, and the metaphysics of St. Thomas Aquinas as much as possible.

In this narrative I constructed in *World*, the Big Bang, a phase change of sorts, can be seen as the beginning of God's acts of shaping something into this universe. I called that something the Primordial Universe and speculated it's a manifestation of the truths God chose for all of Creation. It turns out that others had similar thoughts in recent decades, including Father George Lemaitre, the Catholic priest from Belgium who was co-discoverer of the Big Bang model back in the late 1920s.

The effort to describe and understand the physical aspects of this phase of God's Creation is a scientific problem. Human beings, particularly those of Western Civilization, have taken good advantage of our chances to explore this universe, to describe it, and to understand it. There is no doubt that the vast expansion of scientific knowledge has created great opportunities and dangers for Christian believers.

The opportunities come from a better understanding of this phase of God's Creation and that is the same as a better understanding of God's ways of achieving His purposes for us and for the universe. The dangers come from the difficulty of updating our inherited understanding of our world and from our reluctance to even try. Many have drifted away from the Church, many others have not come towards the Church, because they think falsely that modern science has proven that Christian dogmas are false. It is true that modern science has proven that some of our narrative settings of Christian dogmas are false. In fact, as I showed in *World*, evolutionary theory has shown us that morality has evolved by natural processes. Non-human animals, especially social mammals, have been shown to have strong moral natures. To a great extent, there is a continuity between our moral natures and those of wolves and bears. Man is morally different from his fellow animals not in being moral but rather in being capable of the sort of abstract thought which can allow us to adapt to new circumstances or even to unstable situations. The human capabilities which allow us to develop abstract mathematics or to explore the floor of the ocean are the same capabilities which make us suited to be friends of God.

Heaven is not endangered by modern scientific knowledge, though we can't view it in the same terms as those who lived before Galileo. In my way of telling the story of God's Creation, Heaven is another phase of Creation, shaped from the Primordial Universe. Our universe was also shaped from that Primordial Universe which lies on the other side of the so-called Big Bang, but God shapes Heaven so that it has far different properties than our present universe. I usually refer to it as the world of the resurrected rather than Heaven, but it's basically the same place. That world of the resurrected, Heaven in common language, is the place where Jesus Christ lives with those who are His. It's a place where the Peace of Christ reigns because Christ reigns. It's not a place of development and decay as is this universe, but rather a place where strife has ended and pain and suffering are no more.

We can't go there directly. God will have to resurrect us, recreate us. The only reason we have to be sure it will really be us is the one which comes from the previous section, *What Will be Saved?*. We can be sure that, if we are resurrected, we will really be us because it's God's love that creates and shapes us most completely, though we are also shaped somewhat by the love of other human beings and by the events of our mortal lives. If Joe Smith dies and suddenly a Joe Smith with a perfected body is resurrected into Heaven, he's the same Joe Smith because he's the object of the same personal love which God directed towards the mortal human body of Joe

Smith.

God is in all that exists, bringing it into existence on an ongoing basis. He's in Heaven and He's also on the top of Mt. Everest and down in Death Valley. If He were not in some speck of time or space, it would cease to exist. The rest of us are pretty much stuck where God places us, but our primary nature is that of an object of a particular act of love by God, an act I refer to as an act-of-being in other contexts. So long as that particular act of love is the same, the act that shaped Joe Smith, then Joe will exist where and when God decides to localize that act of love or act-of-being.

## 3.4 Who Will Be Saved?

After telling a story about a woman who'd married seven brothers in turn, some Sadducees asked, "In the resurrection, therefore, whose wife will the woman be?" We read the response:

> And Jesus said to them, "The sons of this age marry and are given in marriage; but those who are accounted worthy to attain to that age and to the resurrection from the dead neither marry nor are given in marriage..." [Luke 20:34 covers the entire incident.]

Perhaps more to the point of this book:

> When Jesus had spoken these words, he lifted up his eyes to heaven and said, "Father, the hour has come; glorify thy Son that the Son may glorify thee, since thou has given him power over all flesh, to give eternal life to all whom thou hast given him. And this is eternal life, that they know thee the only true God, and Jesus Christ whom thou hast sent." [John 17:1-3]

Jesus promised eternal life to those the Father gave to Him. This puts the Lord Jesus Christ squarely in the Biblical prophetic tradition where the choice we face is that between death or true life, a share in the life of God.

> "And this is eternal life, that they know thee the only true God, and Jesus Christ whom thou hast sent." [John 17:3]

This is the resurrection, this is salvation, this is peace: to know the true God and His Son, Jesus Christ. To know God, to accept his offer of friendship is eternal life. How can there be eternal life for those who don't share the life of God?

Why didn't Jesus claim each and every one of us at our conception, as He did with His mother, or at the moment of our first being in His presence, as He did with St. John the Baptist in some traditions of the Church? Why do we have to travel through this valley of tears, as did Mary and John the Baptist, but without being already taken up to the Lord Jesus Christ? That is, why don't we already share the peace of our Lord? Why don't we have the consolations given to Mary and John the Baptist since our troubles are similar to theirs?

Of course, our troubles are not entirely similar to theirs because we share with them the natural troubles of a mortal human life, but few of us have shown any willingness to suffer for what's right and good. As a people we don't even have the integrity to shut off our televisions, to be rid of a corrupt entertainment industry for the sake of our souls and the souls of our children. We don't stay home to repair our domestic affairs and we don't try to reestablish neighborhood life because we've allowed ourselves to be trained to rush about frantically, from store to store to restaurant and then to another store before heading home to catch a couple of hours of shows on the TV. This isn't the way to find even a hint of the Peace of Christ.

Here's the funny part, the part which will upset some but calm those humble before God. Our existence is a gift. Our very bodies are also a gift. It's those bodies which give us some sort of objective existence – with some sort of creaturely independence from God Himself. And, yet, even in our limited creaturely independence, our very existence and our substance is a result of the love God directs our way. The man who exists is a shadowy being defined only by the relationships which God chooses to have with that moral creature. It's the love which God directs our way which is as real as God Himself. But we don't feel that love, we don't even know what or who we really are, so long as we don't seek the quiet in which God's whispering voice can be heard.

We have no power to save ourselves. We have no power to make ourselves suited for life as companions to Jesus Christ. But that doesn't matter. We have the promises of a faithful God that He will save those who love His Son, our Lord Jesus Christ. Will He save others and teach them to love Jesus Christ? We really can't know in this life.

Let us be at peace, knowing that our Creator has the power to save us. When we carry out God's commandments or when we feel a hint of His Presence in our deepest parts, then we can feel confident He's at work. We sin if we become complacent about our salvation. We're bound to work hard in the manner of the athletes used as examples by St. Paul, but we can be at peace even as we work hard.

# 4 Seeking Peace

## 4.1 Do We Need a Self-help Manual?

There are certainly many self-help manuals available in this age where we look for solutions to problems we can't even define. The Bible is the ultimate self-help manual but it's far more than that. It can also help us to define the problems which bother us, leaving us ill at ease in the world into which we were born, the world in which we develop. The key phrase is "help us," because God didn't fully define our problems and certainly didn't solve them. Nor did He even tell us how to go about defining our problems. He left much for us to discover on our own – in particular, we need to explore the universe, this phase of God's Creation to discover what sorts of beings we are and what sort of world this is.

It can be appropriate to write self-help manuals though the best such works would be better labeled as advice to dependent, rational animals. One of the problems with most self-help manuals, even those which try to respect Christian truths, is that they are advice to individualistic, rational animals – and there are no such beasts.

We seek peace properly when we let down our barriers, the ones formed to protect our illusions of an egocentric self. We seek peace properly when we realize that even matter comes into existence by way of relationships. This idea, which I'll not discuss further in this book, is found in the teachings of St. John the Apostle about love. It can also be found in the philosophy and theology of St. Thomas Aquinas. More surprisingly, it's quite consistent with some radical philosophies which attempt to understand the strangeness of quantum mechanics. We achieve peace when we form the proper relationships, accepting truly the love of God and trying to return it in some small measure. We achieve peace when we accept our role in our human communities, families and local political communities and local communities of worship. These smaller and more local communities are foreshadowings of the greater community into which Christ would bind us.

How is this done? What does it mean to form the proper relationships? I'll try to give some insight on these matters in the remaining sections of this chapter. We need faith to understand, and we deepen our faith by deepening our understanding. But a simple faith is fine in those who are willing to rely upon their shepherds. Still is there much that even a simple believer can learn from the hard-won experience of a sinner who has been duped and dragged along by God in the direction of the Peace of Christ.

## 4.2 Prayer

### Why Pray?

The major reason to pray is clear-cut and beyond argument to any Christian: God has told us to pray to Him as part of our meager efforts to render justice to our Maker. But He usually has other reasons for us to obey than just our duties to Him. It would be even more accurate to say that our duties to God and what is good for us are just aspects of God's love for us. We should pray because it makes us more suited to share the life of God. We might even speculate that our prayers are analogous to the ways in which the Persons of the Holy Trinity commune with each other.

But why the ritual, why the intercessionary prayers? God is all-powerful. Does He really gain from the ritual prayers of hairless apes who are tiny, powerless citizens of an awfully big universe? Our Creator knows us better than we know ourselves. He knows what happiness can be ours on the other side of the grave. Does He need to listen to our requests for assistance for ourselves or our fellow creatures?

We can retreat to my first claim:

> God has told us to pray to Him as part of our meager efforts to render justice to our Maker.

There's more to it than this because our Maker does not separate ideals and practical morality the way that our philosophers and theologians will sometimes do. We have little reason to believe He would have bothered to create us solely for the purpose of worshiping Him. He created us out of a pure love and not to gain anything for Himself. What could we give

Him that He needs? There must be something about prayer that helps us to achieve our salvation, helps us to become suited to life without end as companions of God.

There are hints of what this might be in the spiritual writings of great saints such as St. Theresa of Avila (see *The Way of Perfection* as one example) but these hints are partially obscured by the related errors of belief about human beings that lead us to an early form of modern liberalism: the belief that human beings were, and are, created as some sort of autonomous agents possessing free-wills. We're social creatures, each of us heavily dependent upon other human beings and absolutely dependent upon God. From the creaturely point of view, Christ's message – "Convert or perish," – can be restated: We're absolutely dependent upon the Body of Christ and we're also greatly dependent upon each other. Without a conversion, that is – an entrance into the Body of Christ, we'll perish. Many won't like this because they feel that dependency is a weakness to be avoided; they would stand on their own two feet, oblivious to their true situation in this universe. The rest of us can accept our dependency upon others and even see some good in it. Dependency, though seemingly a weakness, forces us into smaller bodies which will become part of the Body of Christ.

## Praying the Psalms

The Psalms had a special role in the prayer and worship of the ancient Hebrews and they still have a special role in the prayer of modern Jews and Christians. From the very first Psalm, we hear of the meaning of a God-centered life:

> Blessed is the man
> who walks not in the counsel of the wicked,
> nor stands in the way of sinners,
> nor sits in the seat of scoffers;
> but his delight is in the law of the Lord,
> and on his law he meditates day and night.
>
> ...

The Psalms teach us how to ask God for help, as in Psalm 6:

> O Lord, rebuke me not in thy anger,

nor chasten me in thy wrath.
Be gracious to me, O Lord, for I am languishing;
O Lord, heal me, for my bones are troubled.
My soul also is sorely troubled.
But thou, O Lord—how long?

...

They teach us how to ask for forgiveness, as in Psalm 51:

Have mercy on me, O God,
according to thy steadfast love;
according to thy abundant mercy blot out my transgressions.
Wash me thoroughly from my iniquity,
and cleanse me from my sin!

For I know my transgressions,
and my sin is ever before me.
Against thee, thee only, have I sinned,
and done that which is evil in thy sight,
so that thou art justified in thy sentence
and blameless in thy judgment.
Behold, I was brought forth in iniquity,
and in sin did my mother conceive me.

...

Then there are the glorious psalms of ascent, such as Psalm 123:

To thee I lift up my eyes,
O thou who art enthroned in the heavens!
Behold, as the eyes of servants
look to the hand of their master,
as the eyes of a maid
to the hand of her mistress,
so our eyes look to the Lord our God,
till he have mercy upon us.

Have mercy upon us, O Lord, have mercy upon us,

for we have had more than enough of contempt.
Too long our soul has been sated
with the scorn of those who are at ease,
the contempt of the proud.

The Psalms played a special role in the worship of the Hebrews for centuries before the birth of Christ. They also played a role in the worship of monks from the earliest centuries of Christianity. In some of the early experiments with a way of praying the Psalms, some monastic orders prayed so frequently and so long as to be able to cover all the Psalms, plus other Biblical readings and prayers, every two weeks or even less.

We don't need to be quite that extreme, but it remains true that the Psalms remain a very important part of the Bible: the most prayerful of the books of Scripture. And so we do well by praying these Psalms, the hymns of David and others of that general period, men who were loved by God in a special way though they were sinners – great sinners in the case of King David. And those men loved God in return.

The western churches of Christianity developed the Psalmody into a regular way of prayer by the early Middle Ages and that is essentially the prayer which is used in monasteries and friaries and is also prayed by priests and deacons. The entire schedule of prayers is called *The Liturgy of the Hours.* Morning prayer, evening prayer, night prayer are the major 'hours' though there are minor hours which lie between between. Morning prayer may also be split into Vigils and Lauds, but most of us will do well by praying the three major hours, even if we can't pray them in their entirety every day.

Check into the various shorter and longer versions of the *The Liturgy of the Hours*, but the real goal is to pray the psalms along with the saints, living and dead. By praying when we need to give thanks, we will remember Who is the source of our very beings and all the good we experience. By praying for forgiveness when we haven't done as we should or when we simply feel mean, we will remember Who it is that can forgive us and also heal us. By praising and giving glory to God, we give to our Maker some small return on His gifts, but small return is all He has asked of us.

If we can't spend some of our hours in this life with God, why would we expect to enjoy spending time without end with Him? How could we expect to enjoy that Peace for time without end on the other side of the grave?

## Simple Prayers

By simple prayers, I mean only the conversations we should be having with God as we go about our business each day. Such a prayer can be so simple as, "Thank you, Lord," when an irresponsible or distracted driver narrowly misses us in a crosswalk. It can be a reminder repeated, silently or under the breath or more loudly, as we're walking about or reading a book or doing some chores: "Lord Jesus Christ, have mercy on me a sinner." We can praise God for a beautiful Spring day or for the sight of playful children: "You do good work, Lord God Almighty."

We don't always need elaborate routines or elegant prayers from the Bible or the books of a spiritual writer. Those can be important, but remember God is giving us a chance to be friends and companions of His Son, through Him friends and companions to the Father and the Holy Spirit as well. We should talk to God sometimes as if we were already friends of His.

We can also talk to the saints or even those who might be saints. We should think of our relationships with our mothers, or maybe the relationships we wish we'd had, and then let the Mother of God adopt us. We should talk to Mary and also to our own mothers. We should talk to our birthday saints and our confirmation or baptismal saints. We should talk to one of the crazy saints – there are more than a few and they're usually amusing to read about. We should certainly talk to our holy and departed grandmothers or maybe our grouchy uncles who might well be missing from Heaven unless there's plenty to drink up there. Prayer of this sort is conversation and not the sort of prayer we raise up to God, though we might ask the saints or our departed loved ones to pray to God for us.

Let us pray for our parents' forgiveness for the many times we strayed and they protected us or brought us back from the depths. Even then we should remember it's God's forgiveness that matters in the truest way, but we were invited into the community of saints. We're not to be a huge mob of individuals milling about Heaven, each talking only to God.

The saints are living in the Peace of Christ. Let them help us also to enter.

## Intercessionary Prayers

God knows what we need before we do. In fact, we may never – in this life – know what we truly need. It's hard to think this way, but we might need to pass through suffering and pain before we reach the Peace of Christ and we might even pass through those dark regions for the good of others, such as children who've strayed from God and His Church.

So maybe we should never pray for help? Or maybe we should never pray for specific help? Should we pray only, "Give us our daily bread and let Your will be done."?

I don't think that would be wise for most human beings. It's far better to remain aware of our needs and to ask God for help in meeting those needs. The proper sort of abandonment would come from regular evaluations of those needs, with the help of a spiritual guide if possible. Remember that God knows better than we do what we need. We need to enter the conversation with God that He might begin to tell us what we need. Let our Maker ratchet down our desires and our estimates of our needs if proper. Again, a spiritual guide can often help us to speak with God.

## Contemplative Prayer

When we've said all we need to say, when we've asked for our basic needs and for assistance for the troubled creatures of this world, then it's time for us to sit quietly. The spiritual masters tell us we must grow accustomed to being in God's Presence. I would change that a little: we must grow accustomed to being aware that we're in God's Presence. After all, God is He who gives existence not only to men but also to rocks and stars and magnetic fields. Where anything exists, even a seemingly empty region of space and time, God is there. If God were not there then that place and that time would cease to exist. We're in God's Presence, during the good times and bad times of our lives. We don't need to move into that Presence but only to become aware that we're already there.

Sometimes, we might find ourselves aware of God's Presence, perhaps at Mass or at the baptism of a screaming child. After such an experience, we can be frightened to find out that it remains hard to be aware of God's Presence as we go about each and every activity, as we live each and every second of our lives. Would we sin so readily if we were truly aware that God is with us even as we steal or commit adultery, as we take His name in vain, as we misuse our talents or the other resources in our environments?

Let us sit quietly and let the awareness of God's Presence come upon us. He'll take care of things.

Once we're aware of God's Presence, we'll begin to realize that the Lord God Almighty is quietly present inside of us and not just in the grand events and glorious things of Creation. There will be no more than a whisper which lets us know He's there.

We should sit quietly and learn to listen along with God, to speak along with God, to think along with God.

In this is found the Peace of Christ: to realize that our Creator brings us into existence at each and every instant, that He is the energy behind all that we do even when we exercise the creaturely freedom with which He gifted us. We must always be aware of our absolute and utter dependence upon our Maker.

## 4.3 Community Worship

God calls each of us as individuals, but He calls us into the Body of Christ. In this life, He calls us to join the pilgrim Church as she stumbles along in Her creaturely way.

Nature formed the human species as a social species, a species in which the individual exists in a stable and secure form only inside of the proper social relationships. God created us by first loving us. This love of individual creatures doesn't create from nothing but it shapes those creatures from the stuff of this universe. We're also shaped by our interactions with our environments, including the other human beings around us. We're shaped and we shape others.

Proper shaping of our beings results from love. We must love others and accept their love. This is our duty to God – to help Him tell a story brought into being by His love for us.

We're creatures who are objects of relationships and not freestanding individuals. We're objects of God's love and this is not the same as: we exist and then God chose to love us. No, God chose to love us and we came into being as objects of His love.

God's acts of creating each of us are many from the creaturely viewpoint but we can think of these stages:

- God created the basic stuff of all Creation from nothing;
- He shaped the universe out of that basic stuff;
- He shaped the human race during billions of years of evolution of life on earth; and
- He shapes each of us from the time of our conception until the time of our death and will continue to shape His friends after death until they're prepared to live with His Son for time without end.

The Lord God Almighty has shaped the human race as a social species, a species which has an evolutionary past which tells us we live best in tight-knit extended families or tribes, so-called nuclear families bound together under common leadership – perhaps a patriarch or a chieftain or a council of elders. From the human viewpoint, we were made to be bonded into social groups before we become true friends of God. And we can become friends of God only by being very tightly bonded into the Body of Christ, the Church.

We become tightly bonded into the Body of Christ first and foremost by worshiping in Christian communities. The picnics and the Bible study groups, the gathering of food for the poor and the spreading of the Good News to the lonely, are all important, even necessary to a Christian community. But it all begins when we gather for the two parts of a Christian worship service:

- First, we hear the Word of the Lord; and
- Second, we gather around the table of the Lord's Supper, the Eucharist which is the greatest of all Thanksgiving meals.

The Peace of Christ is to be found there, in the communities which will one day come together to form the complete and perfect Body of Christ. I'll not deny that all of us can be irritants to others when we gather for worship or to organize a fundraiser or to help the poor or sick. Learning how to deal with each other is also a part of entering the Peace of Christ.

# 5 The Peace That Sustains Itself

## 5.1 Meeting the World

And how are we to sustain the Peace of Christ as we lead our lives in a world so hectic as ours? Our eyes and ears are under constant assault and our brains work hectically to gather together a coherent stream of thought. Many seem to give up, so far as I can tell, allowing themselves to drift as flotsam upon the currents of a culture which resembles a raging flood filled with rubbish. It's not a steady river of the sort that could allow orderly human lives to be lived by those moving into the future.

How can we be at peace in such a world, so dangerous to our minds and souls? The danger is far greater just because we've made great progress in easing certain dangers to our physical being. We've also advanced technologically but we've used much of our technology to develop highways and motor vehicles which have destroyed our social and moral environments while also severely damaging our physical environments. Highways and motor vehicles are just one example of many morally dangerous uses of modern technology.

None of this makes for peace in our environments. And we have to always remember that we live in small-scale environments and human communities before we live in a gargantuan nation. We even live in those environments and communities before we live in God's world and before we live in the pilgrim Church.

Our social and moral and physical environments are stressed greatly, damaged or even destroyed far too often. While some are called to quiet lives of praying for the rest of us and for all of God's world, most are called to lead lives 'in the world' as the phrase goes. To lead such an active life leaves us twisting about on fragile rafts which largely move at the mercy of those turbulent currents of our period of history.

And yet we are called to be in a state of peace, the Peace of Christ, in our innermost selves as we are tossed from side to side, even as we are sometimes tossed into the currents or have to watch loved ones being tossed into those currents.

There's no great secret to this. We can only pray and worship and wait for God to establish this peace inside of us. The Peace that surpasses all understanding truly belongs to Christ and only He can give it to us, only He can sustain that Peace inside of us.

## 5.2 Listening and Thinking Along With God

We should listen but not listen for God to speak to us. We should be more aware of His Presence. We might find ourselves listening along with God, and then we'll notice something odd. As St. Thomas Aquinas predicted, we'll find that we're also thinking along with God. It'll be an experience that will come and go. Let us turn ourselves over to God, He'll be working for us but we'll find He'll step back as if He were a wise mother helping her children to learn how to walk. Painfully scraped knees are part of that process of learning how to walk.

This is salvation. Not to go to some Disneyland where God entertains us for eternity and not to lose our own selves by eternal absorption into God. Salvation is to live in that Presence of God so that He can give us not only true life but also true freedom.

The Bible tells us that we gain true life by giving up our life. We also gain true freedom by doing just as God commanded. These are not paradoxes but rather statements which help us make a imaginative journey from this world to the world of the resurrected. They are statements which help to prepare us to live in that better world. Theologians in the Christian tradition have often started by first doing negative theology to discipline thoughts of God, first denying that we can make absolutely true statements about God based upon our creaturely knowledge. My favorite example is "God is simple." That statement is a seeming paradox that makes us first think of God as being some sort of homogeneous gloppy mass, but that itself is a creaturely way of thought. We have to stop thinking of God in terms of creaturely substance, and any substantial body of negative theology will try to remove that error as well. In fact, to think properly as a Christian, a man or woman has to agree to have many of their most basic assumptions removed since those assumptions are appropriate only for creaturely being. To return to my example, the statement "God is simple," is a denial that God has parts in the way of a creature and a denial that He changes in the way of creatures.

The statement, "We must surrender our lives to find true life," is intended to prepare us for that surrender to God so that He might give us greater possibilities than we have in this mortal life lived amidst growth and development but also decay and death. The statement, "We must surrender our false freedom to find true freedom," serves a similar purpose.

As St. Augustine of Hippo said, "The man who truly loves God can do as he will." This is because that God-centered man will do as God would have Him do. Since God alone has perfect freedom, this is to act along with God in His freedom.

Only God has a truly free will. Only God can act in a truly random way, that is, to bring about an event of zero probability such as to create from nothing. Even the shaping of this universe from some sort of more general stuff involved an initial state that had so low a probability that it leaves scientists confused and leaves the pagans among them looking for a way of viewing that low-probability state as one which couldn't have been otherwise.

To surrender our lives and our paltry freedoms to God is to gain a share of that divine life and that divine freedom. For God is merciful. He brought men into existence that He might enjoy our companionship for time without end. After all, we were made that His Son might become one of us.

We know not how many men will pass on to true life and how many will simply enter the grave as a place of final and absolute death or perhaps be cast into a region of pain without end. But we know the Almighty Creator wants friends to populate the world of the resurrected. We can even presume that a true surrender to His will, an offering up of our lives and our paltry freedoms, will more than satisfy Him. He may have to do much more to prepare us for that true life and true freedom, and those preparations might be painful, but we can have faith He will take unto Himself those who are trying hard to be His friends.

This is another way to speak of the Peace of Christ:

We find ourselves in the Peace of Christ when we offer ourselves to God and have faith that He will accept our voluntary offering of that which already belongs to Him. It will be a more pleasing sacrifice than the greatest of holocausts ever offered on the altars of the Temple of Jerusalem.

# Colophon

This manual was typeset using the LaTeX typesetting system written by Leslie Lamport and the memoir class written by Peter Wilson. The body text is set 10/12pt on a 33pc measure with Computer Modern Roman designed by Donald Knuth. Other fonts include Sans, Smallcaps, Italic, Slanted and Typewriter, all from Knuth's Computer Modern family.